*To Heather,
with affection.

Randy
1/15/07*

RANDALL J. VanderMey

A POETIC DRAMA IN FIVE PARTS

FIVE WOMEN OF THE ODYSSEY

ARTAMO PRESS

SANTA BARBARA · CALIFORNIA

Published by
ARTAMO PRESS

First edition, 2006
Copyright © 2006 by Randall J. VanderMey

Artamo Press is a division of Artamo LLC.

Book and cover design by Jack N. Mohr

Library of Congress Control Number: 2006933902
ISBN-13: 978-0-9788475-2-4
ISBN-10: 0-9788475-2-0

www.artamopress.com

Printed on acid-free paper in the United States of America

With heartfelt thanks to
    John Blondell, for the prompt
    Robert Fagles, for sounding Homer in my ear
    Pam Kuhlken, for over-the-top support
    Jack N. Mohr and Monika Laskowski-Caujolle,
    for your vision

And with faithful love and thanks to
    Dana, my Penelope, my new moon

I.
CIRCE: MEN ARE PIGS

Come, my primitive little ship's captain, you've not touched your food. Do you not approve of its arrangement on the plate? We call this *nouvelle cuisine...* that's French.

So sullen. Did I say "little"? It was the ship I meant. Surely you are built on a more... impressive scale. I imagine you could bench press one of my guardian wolves.

My burly, bearded little man — is that all *you* — the hams, the hocks, such potential, ... oh my. I'm sure I could provide you with incentives to keep working out. I love the smell of a gym. And the grunting. When I hear all that grunting and clanging, I know that no great harm is being done elsewhere. Raw eggs, protein powder, creatine, glutamine, branched chain amino acids, ooo. I love my men vascular, hard, and ultra-ripped! You will find that the new supplements work "magic"! They will look so good on you. All natural. None of that 'roid rage. And none of those unfortunate... little "acorns."

I like silent men. They fill me with a sense of power. I like to watch them eat. I like to prepare what they eat.

Why don't you eat.

ODYSSEUS

After my men.

CIRCE

Your men. Your little men. How touching. Though usually it's the "father" who... sniffs the cork.

Let me assure you, your charming crew will be present at our little feasts. In fact, they would "squeal" with anticipation if they knew what was cooking.

Your men are quite happy... being themselves. I've seen no essential alteration in them.

Your concern?

ODYSSEUS

What is with —

CIRCE

Circe. C - I - R - C - E... *not* French...

ODYSSEUS

Circe, then. *What is with the* — ... walkway, front yard, the —

CIRCE

— heads on posts?

ODYSSEUS

Y-yes. The munching goats.

CIRCE

The little piggies?!

ODYSSEUS

The free range chickens. It's weird. The stench. Come on. Reminded me of something —

9

                              CIRCE

Colonel Kurtz?

                            ODYSSEUS

Yes!

                              CIRCE

I saw the movie. Decorative touch.

                            ODYSSEUS

Of course… *Flores por los muertos… flores por los muertos…*

                              CIRCE

No no no no no. That's Albee.

                            ODYSSEUS

Right!

                              CIRCE

Theater. Magic!

You are a very confused man. You must be very tired. Jealous
gods and their stupid kids — edible flowers that steal every
desire for wife and home — never a good thing — flesh-
eating giants — running running, rowing rowing. This is
life? Albee! Horrible. Perhaps your memory's running on
reserve tank. You must be getting sleepy. You're getting very
very sleepy.

Tell you what. You won't eat?

Steward!

Let me pour you a little… something. A little pickme up, a wee dram. And to bring out the *animal* in you, a little something from the garden, roots up from where the Dark Mother dwells, a little couch grass, some jezebel root, mugwort, lady's thumb, and to top it off, some delicious GHB… Stir… I call this a "Sleeping Beauty." You will call it "Surcease of Sorrow."

Reach out your hand, sir. I do not bite.

Yes, now swallow… swallow… very good.

As you feel the drift begin — think of your ship at sea, Poseidon's restless hand under your keel — now turn upon me the fading sunset of your mortal mind. Answer me in the intimacy of this moment, now before you fall upon all four and run squealing to the wallow, to the place of your dreams, a world without women:

Do I look as if I were one who could be reduced to my… parts? Would you pronounce the word "bimbo," sir?

How old do you think me to be? You may guess and guess again, and again and again… my pet…

What is this?

ODYSSEUS

[*Belch*]

CIRCE

Powers of the Pentagram! Why do you tarry…?

ODYSSEUS

Not bad.

CIRCE

Suffering Mother of Persephone!

ODYSSEUS

Do you have this in a Lite? Something less filling…

CIRCE

No man has yet withstood — Unless Zeus — No man —

ODYSSEUS

Indeed, "No Man" — Ravager of Cities. I am he.

CIRCE

Would you smile?!

ODYSSEUS

You read me well.

CIRCE

You are then that Odysseus, of whom legend —

ODYSSEUS

Prepare to die! By the power of Zeus,…

CIRCE

Put up your sword!

ODYSSEUS

Through Hermes craft, by which I clutch this *moly*,

CIRCE

Moly!

ODYSSEUS

proof against your poisons and your spells, by which thus I
proof this sword against the corrosives in your *blood*!

CIRCE / ODYSSEUS
[*simultaneously*]

[*Screams*] / Let it fall!

CIRCE

Hold! Hold! What would you have?

ODYSSEUS

Your life!

CIRCE

I am immortal. You cannot take it.

ODYSSEUS

No, but I could make it pretty miserable.

CIRCE

What would you have that I can give?

ODYSSEUS

Your power, your book, the pleasure of your bed.

CIRCE

I am yielded. I lay down my book. What more?

ODYSSEUS

Free my men from infernal bondage.

CIRCE

There is nothing to restore.

ODYSSEUS

They are not swine.

CIRCE

I swear, I've done nothing by magic but remove the veil.
Check it out. You see now as woman —

ODYSSEUS

Even so!

CIRCE

Done. Done! Let them appear as men. Nothing altered

[*They filter in, bewildered, scratching themselves.*]

ODYSSEUS

See that they are fed.

CIRCE

Oh, they have well fed. They have done nothing but feed,
these rooting and rutting disciples of yours.

ODYSSEUS

Very well then. The god has answered my prayer, in all things but one.

CIRCE

One?

ODYSSEUS

Your kiss. Be mindful of my sword. I would have no sorcery but the sorcery of your lips.

CIRCE

In the dark.

ODYSSEUS

You would bargain with this blade?

CIRCE

My kiss is one thing your muscled arm cannot compel. Scum of manly battle, player with toys, collector of badges and bottle caps,… you know nothing of a woman's power.

ODYSSEUS

It is undimmed memory of a woman's virtue, my trust in her trust, that draws me home, though my house be leveled for a strip mall, though my bed be defiled by pigs. As my queen has always said to me, with wisdom from above: "Blessed are those who expect nothing, for they shall not be disappointed." I expect nothing. I have lost every ship but my own, and all men but these, these… feeders, who neglect the fitting sacrifice. What is left of my

15

wife? How can I know? I expect nothing. If she lives to greet me at my door, what might I embrace: botox, liposuction, collagen, Lasik surgery, tummy tucks, water bras (a touch of the sea)… I expect nothing. Yet I live in hope such as you cannot conceive. I would crawl ashore naked and broken, if it came to that. I would crawl to my queen on bloody knees! Such is my hope.

Do I know *nothing*, then, of a woman's power? Who are *your* partners — boy toys drugged out of their gourds? Skulls on popsicle sticks?

CIRCE

Yet you seek my kiss.

ODYSSEUS

My head swirls. A riptide sucks me from shore…

Is this your magic, Sorceress?

I will cling to the raft of my hope!

CIRCE

Odysseus, you will have your wife, once more. You may trust this more-than-mortal word. And she will be beautiful,… for her age. And your son, Telemachus, who's a little socially tweaked — no father, you know — but a good kid overall, in the B+ range, student government, social committee, you get the picture,… he'll be waiting. There's somebody to run the store about the time you start forgetting to zip up or flush, you know what I mean.

And you will have my kiss.

ODYSSEUS

Don't play with me.

CIRCE

No play. This is business. You will have me.

ODYSSEUS

But how?

CIRCE

You will find out. In the dark.

ODYSSEUS

But how? I mean, how will I return? Tell me what you know.

CIRCE

You will find out. In the dark.

ODYSSEUS

Trust you? In the dark? Beguiling singer, weaver of schemes, mixer of drinks: I can't trust you under the all-revealing sun. Imagine, swordless in the dark.... I would soon be swordless indeed.

CIRCE

I promise I would leave you twice the man.

ODYSSEUS

Do you swear?

17

CIRCE

I swear by all that's holy. I swear by my braids. I swear by the book. I swear like a sailor. Odysseus, look me in the eye: "Girl Scout's honor." Would you have me swear more?

ODYSSEUS

Hermes works for me.

CIRCE

And for me.

ODYSSEUS

I cannot do it, deep as I desire.

CIRCE

Would you see Penelope again?

ODYSSEUS

Hope alone, trust and a vision of peace, draws this man of war to my home, to my bed, to the best that mortal love affords.

CIRCE

I hold the key to that hope.

ODYSSEUS

In the darkness of your kiss?

CIRCE

Through the darkness of my kiss to a still deeper darkness.

But first, a year you must remain. For you and your men, a year will vanish in the joy of a feast. With you alone, I will feast.

ODYSSEUS

I cannot.

CIRCE

Would you see Penelope again?

ODYSSEUS

Your words are dark enough. What is this "deeper darkness"?

CIRCE

Your journey must lead through the Kingdom of the Dead — Hermes gives it out. Psychopompos? Guide of Souls? Yes. He will lead you through. Bring your little sprig of *moly*, toxic to all mortal touch. He will spare your hand. And it will save your scalp.

Get up off the floor, muscle man. You fear the softness of my bed? You fear my dark? More greatly fear the bed of death, the kiss of pale eternity. What stroke of sword can separate bloodless shade from shade?

Do you want to be a hero? That's where heroes go.

Now get up.

Let's get you washed and oiled.

The glorious sun is setting.

ODYSSEUS

Why to death, where accident and treachery and false pride lead? Why should love, too, lead me there, and hope, and trust, all effort, and zeal? All blastings off and landings? Is an epic, then, more than a long, long fall? I'm climbing a hill here. My home is at the top. My wife. My love. I worship Zeus, not Sisyphus. Must I roll down with the rock of mortal grief for good?

CIRCE

Note, oh man of many wiles and many tears, what I said: *through* the Dead, not down to Death. Not yet. You'll live to trip the light fantastic. Among the dead, you will meet the ghost of blind Tiresias, seer of Thebes.

ODYSSEUS

The one who knows of things to come?

CIRCE

It's his job. He alone among the shades.

He will tell you how the journey runs. The date and state and means of your return.

ODYSSEUS

He in whom man and woman mingled be? He of the wrinkled dugs?

CIRCE

He's got a great personality.

Meanwhile, Odysseus, come, may I offer you something more, gratifying?

I have made my offer. You know the terms.

ODYSSEUS

A year?

CIRCE

Tops.

ODYSSEUS

Will Penelope be waiting?

CIRCE

She won't be on her swingset, mind you. There's stuff for her to do. Life isn't easy, with Telemachus, a teenager, all this carousing in the mead hall, feeding the dogs — you know. I'm saying this as a woman. A goddess. But I don't know everything. That's why, Tiresias.

ODYSSEUS

My men —

CIRCE

Your men. There're going to eat like you wouldn't believe.

And you're the one who gets dessert.

Deal?

ODYSSEUS

A year.

CIRCE

Girl Scouts' honor.

II.
CALYPSO, RIDING

Above me is Calypso, riding,
bending over me, pulling me up, the amorous nymph,
she of the braided hair,
night after night, for seven years, years of days washed by my
weeping,
down on the sea strand, watching the clashings of surf for news
that never comes, news of home, 11 o'clock news of the peril-
ous voyage
back to the man I am.

She ceases to delight me, she of the immortal arms and braided hair.

Perfect bliss

is an island — nothing happens here.
All the waves that gallop toward us gnashing
from the caves of wind
die on the beaches all around. I pick up coconuts
and hack at their cordy husks. Nothing
is here to be built. No use for my muscled arm.
Nothing to wall out.

Penelope!

I want to be burnished in use
like Seamus Heaney's scoop, sunk past my gleam in a
mealbin,
not to rust in my sheath. I will never tell you this —

there are no words for what I must say —

but
nightly in the deeper night of nibbling lips
entangled in the weave of her unbraided hair
I turn on my soul's side and stare at the wall.

                              Penelope!

Heaven grant me even your angry back.
Grant me just a bilious reprimand, as long as it's from you.
Heaven grant me a long lifetime of wrinkling
and smoothing hurts, or balancing checkbooks or
                    swearing
not to drink again, of making ends meet,
of sweeping entryways at your request
before the arrival of guests. Heaven grant me
shrinking equities and workmen's compensation
and bedside visits to dying neighbors,
all the stirring together into one bowl
of cracked grains and sugars, waters, salts, and yeasts.
      I will accept extended dying for life
      and living unto death
            as eternity enough.

                  Will you wait for me, Penelope?
                  I am coming,
                  even if I die.

            When it's time for me to push off
from fragrant, mild Ogygia, toward you, my patient
            weaver,
I will accept the provisions of Calypso's love — the planks

and lashings, the hard tack, the casks of wine.
      Yes, memory will feed on my first sight of her deep
          cave,
the fragrance of blazing juniper and tender arborvitae
wafting through the air, in the grotto her golden shuttle
adding its hum to her graceful song. The entrance wreathed
with vines and their burdens of grape;
bending alders and poplars and pungent cypress
home for the owl and cormorants, gannets and gulls,
all with homes and busy tasks to ply
in the foamy surge. In that way I'll hold
in my soul's dark grotto
the secret of divinity.   But then,

I will hear her shrill complaint to Hermes, courier and
psychopompos — in effect, this: You bastard men
who settle upon such women
as you please. We are like food to you — pigs!
But if a goddess beds a man, hungry for the *one* bliss — rank,
imperfect, mortal bliss — the one that outsweats your
          divine
eternal summer, goddamit, then you're right there
with your lightning bolts. Don't you just love to stand
          around
the barbecue with hands in your pockets. Or when rosy-
fingered Dawn embraced Orion
you sent that virgin archer, Artemis — one of our own —
to impale him on her shafts.

      What is more frightening to you
          than a woman's joy!?

Answer me! This one's mine. I found him.
I dried him off
and buffed him up. He's mine.
How like a little human girl she'll sound to me then,
and I will not be loath to leave.
                                        Only in this
as I press the mothering bosom of the sea, sprawled
upon my planks, only in this
will I carry with me the image of a woman, that she
at last will take as her own will
the will of him whose will cannot be denied: Father God.

Having felt the burden of His word, she will let me go,
bright and free with sweetness of her blessings. And so I,
free after seven years of weeping and nightly sighs,
will sleep with her one last dark night, free under God,
                                        Penelope,
and fit for you, faithful
as I have ever been.

III.
NAUSICAA:
TOSS AND CATCH

Young lady with the white arms of a goddess and the cheek
                    bones and Paul Mitchell hair
of a queen-to-be, surely when you came down to the shore
                    to pound the grease
out of your father's shirts and spread them between rocks to
                    flap dry
while you played, the last thing you and these *cholas* with you
                    thought to see
was me, buck naked, shaking loose from the grip of death and
                    rising
like some dirtball Yeti from a mound of leaves. But here I am,
                    unbeknownst to you
a king.

          Nakedness, be my disguise.
          Let the fair Athena dress me fairly
          in the eyes of the wide world's most fair.

Catch! young lady. Here's your wayward ball.

I see you do not shrink from me. You've been praying for a
                    man, have you.
You've dreamed yourself striding through the popcorn butter
                    light
beneath a movie marquee, hushing young studs in their silly
                    wifebeaters and tattoos;
and yet you've prayed for more: your twelve-point buck, your
                    King.
I see it in your eyes. But now you spy my leathered hide, my
                    bloody knuckles, the breakers
rolling in my stare —

You may wonder if you've prayed too hard.
Be careful for what you pray, is all I can say.
Of all my men I've been the one most dutiful
            in prayer.
You'll notice they're all pushing daisies now.

Toss!

Immortal Law has rolled Its ball down among my reeds time
            and time again.
I've kicked it back, I've sat on it and watched tv,
I've lain on my back and hoisted it with flippers like a circus
            seal, and here I am,
a tangle of dry kelp, a yanked-out holdfast jumping with fleas.
I've woken to so many giggles, screams and cries.
                        Look upon the reeds.
See how they bend, tips to the lipping wave,
how they cut their tiny circles in the sand? So am I
bent to the very line between to be
and not to be.
            Believe me, I've been dreaming of my Queen.

Catch!

This is what I know:
Death is troubled by the dream of life, as life is troubled by
            a dream of death.
To be home, undivided by desire,
that's the dream. Even boundless Ocean dreams of home,
and so under moon and sun alike it reaches, yearning, up
toward Mt. Olympus, pitches down

toward Tartarus. Feast and feces, sun and shade, music and
                    cacophony:
ceaselessly it thrashes toward the end.
And so I've thrashed, like a skate rat in a half-pipe, 19 years
                    from home.

                    Where is home — is it Ithaca or Bust?
                    Wherever at the end my blood drools into sand?
                    Or wherever story, dance, and song spark up
                        the night sky?
I sigh for you, young beauty,
how I sigh. Let me tell you why.

Toss!

Someday so far from now it stirs like mythic memory in my
                    dream
a space shuttle will hurtle from the sky in flame — don't ask
                    what a «space shuttle» is or why it fell or how;
                    it doesn't matter now —
Zeus would be proud of such a fiercely hurtling fire.
A U.S. President — don't ask — will say:
                    The same Creator who names the stars also knows
                        the names
                    of the seven souls we mourn today.
                    The crew of the shuttle Columbia did not return
                    safely to Earth, yet we can pray
                    that all are safely home

Safely home.

Sweet beauty, seek your suitor, he who answers best your
                    queenly charms.
You could be the waiting wife,
Or you could be that astronaut who offers up her life.

Catch!

Go to your father. Leave me some threads. Trust me: I will
                    appear at your door.
My Protector will wrap me in a cloud sarong
until with arms about Alcmene's knees, I cast myself on her
                    mercy's shore.
When the blind bard Demodocus sings of ancient war,
Alcinous will know by my tears that I, your beggared guest,
                    am the subject of his song,
the man with the plan — the Horse, of course! — who used
                    wit's point to blind the strong.

And when your father will have stuffed his flying ship's net
with gifts of skins, and plate, and electronic gizmos beyond
                    measure,
wave to my vanishing sails from this quiet cove, your game
                    face set.
Your flying ship won't return — that's the thanks you'll get.
And I'll seek Penelope, my heart, my home, my truest treasure,
and seek truce with Poseidon, who seems to smack me around
                    for his pleasure.

IV.
DRAWING ON ATHENA

Gray-eyed goddess! Target me, I pray, as I stretch this mighty bow.
Woman warrior, you who sprang in full war cry and dressed
          to kill
from Zeus's brow, help me now.

Twelve ax-heads to split with one straight shaft. And a bow
          that takes
the measure of a man. See how the muscle of my youth springs
in it; see how my own bow now stretches me.

Gray-eyed goddess, girl of a soldier's dreams, pinball pinup
          packing steel,
be real to me now, as the string sings beside my straining cheek.
Come to me, first lady of war. Give me heart where limbs
          would fail.
Hear how my salted sinews shriek!

Ricochets of laughter. A hundred local pricks and princes
diss my homeless look; they're hammered on the dwindling
          stores
of my wine. They'd cash my IRA's. They'd pry off my front
          door.
I begin to see what my wife's 19 years of patient weaving has
          been for.

Come to me, goddess, o softest touch. Stand with all sweet-
          ness and excellence
here in my fingers' fork. Pull with me steadily, steadily,
as when on Ithaca's rock shore, my Phaeacian treasure stowed,
I stood in mist of tears
drawing steadily, steadily,
power from your gaze.

You came first as a water meter reader with strangely royal grace.
You brightened when I fell to your knees, lost and sore.
You named our misted little patch of soil "Ithaca" and laughed
to hear the wily weaving of my words — I would do anything
but let you touch the pounding of my heart. But when you
                    touched me
with your hand, Shape-shifter, there you stood,
taller than woman, more beauteous than she,
more skilled than any woman, even mine, at weaving
wondrous webs. Two sly veterans, we high-fived,
and I stood taller than myself. There were brutes
and brooding menaces, in heaven as on earth, but what could
                    not two
such as we, a mortal soul and the soul's highest joy,
do against them? In secret, pretense fell away.
And in your eyes, veils lifted. Steadily, steadily drawing, I knew.
Here I was, after 19 long years. Home, almost. One blood-
                    bath more.
And so we wove this plan.

Goddess of domestic arts, desirer and worker for everlasting
                    peace,
steady the clonus in my hand, as I turn my beggar's aim
with the dragging sweep of a minute hand toward the proud-
                    est in the hall.

What will a hundred ruby faces be to twelve ax heads
when I have had my way?

Goddess, teach my tentative but faithful son,
waiting in the wings with a faithful swineherd and a goatherd

and a keeper of the cattle, hording there the bragging and
belching
suitors' blades, waiting for the moment when childhood will
end,
teach him how a man makes war. Teach him someday
the ways of a woman, the mystery of the hearth's flame,
the order of a city, and the time for pouring out the blood
of bulls.
May he live to learn it.
Spare him, if you will, knowledge
of the deepest darkness and monotony of waves.

Now goddess, daughter of Zeus, I await your filling of this hall
with holy fire. When it comes, I will release this trembling thread.
Then will I be home to my Penelope. Then will absence fall away.
May she see, in throats shot through, brains splattered on the
floor,
and chandeliers pulled down, what time cannot obscure.
In beggar's weeds, I am the *reductio ad absurdum* of her life.
Suit me for her love, o power divine, o patroness, my lucky charm.

And now,
every breath is held in thrall —
can a legend step out of a ratty RV?
I feel more calm than I should be.

I see your lightning gather.

Let it fall!

V.
PENELOPE/ODYSSEUS: PILLOW TALK

PENELOPE

What are you pointing at? I was practically asleep.

ODYSSEUS

I'm not pointing. I'm blocking one eye, tracking the moon.

PENELOPE

Oh, for heaven's sake. Twenty years ago, wasn't it you dropping right off to sleep? I'd have a cigarette lit and want to tell you about my day, and you, the sweat was hardly dry and you'd already be snoring. I used to think: what will the two of us be like in twenty years?

Put your arms around me, soldier.

ODYSSEUS

Look. The old moon gives way to the new.

PENELOPE

Good omen. But sister moon already looks tired.

ODYSSEUS

I'm aligning my hand with that telephone pole — perfectly still. I used to do that sometimes when I'd come ashore from the pitching boat. Something fixed, unchanging… unbelievable! When I stretched to reach it, I could feel that it was my heart so fiercely pitching. And that's when I would think of you: my north star, unreachable, unchanging. I would think of you as forever the keeper of "us".

PENELOPE

And you were my comet: ever-returning, ever-leaving.

ODYSSEUS

Sometimes I would call out your name.

PENELOPE

Sometimes I would curse yours. But then I would bless you and curse war, and I battered the gods nightly with my prayers. Your old nurse held me together. She's a *wonderful* woman. Jeesh.

ODYSSEUS

But then… marvelous! As I held my breath, eclipsing the moon, I would see the tiniest spark of an edge, then the thinnest white edge, then a brilliant, fattening white arc. I'd see the moon sailing. And suddenly I would know the power of God. All things were wheeling — rams, and bulls, wagons, flying horses, great Orion and seven dancing sisters. I was seeing — and feeling — the very circling of heaven. That gave me strength. Perhaps, someday if I kept burning the rich thigh bones of oxen and pouring out libations for the gods, heaven's circling would lead me to you.

PENELOPE

And so it did.

Sleep now?

ODYSSEUS

Something greater is happening. I have been watching and watching, and the moon has not moved in a full hour.

PENELOPE

Have we a problem?

ODYSSEUS

No, we are witnesses to a great wonder.

Our grey-eyed Protector, the warrior goddess, of many disguises, who pleads for us at the foot of Zeus, stretches and softens the bed of night. She is holding back Blaze and Aurora, the windswift horses of dawn. She has always been at my side.

PENELOPE

Nicely spoken — but that place is taken.

ODYSSEUS

She is overhead. She fills this room. Can't you feel her blessing upon us?

PENELOPE

I feel it through you, when you hug me.

How do you know her?

ODYSSEUS

We have often made war together. She goads me, and when I show courage and faith, she aids me. Did you think it was by my might alone that I strung my ancient bow? By our son's might that he dismissed you from the hall with so manly a gesture, or by your own weakness that you slept through the death groans of a hundred dismembered men? Lookit: these biceps and triceps, these delts, abs, quads, glutes, they're the stuff of legend. Sure, I've suffered for what I've got, but do you really think it was me alone wasting those bad boys? A hundred to one? Well, one and a half, counting Telemachus, Eumaeus and the goatherd…

PENELOPE

Odysseus… cool it. You're home. Love me. Love *me*.

Where are you going?

ODYSSEUS

I have slain monsters for you.

PENELOPE

Good job. Fantastic.

ODYSSEUS

You make light of my trials.

PENELOPE

I have prayed for you, nightly. I have had trials of my own.

Come back under these covers where it's warm.

… plus, I know you so well.

ODYSSEUS

Household economy, weaving, serving roast lamb…

PENELOPE

… raising *our* son, trying to be strong…

ODYSSEUS

… dressing to impress…

PENELOPE

Ridiculous. I held strong. What is this about?

ODYSSEUS

… parties, parties, more parties. Our estate dwindling. Find the new suitor before beauty's petal falls… !

PENELOPE

OH! OH!

ODYSSEUS

Well?…

PENELOPE

There it is. Oh, my God.

ODYSSEUS

My job has been to put a roof over your head, protect you, —

And where was that protection?

— *and* to save a nation. *And* to secure our greater fortune
— for *you*...

I suffered ten, twenty years...

And to steer my hundred foolish sailors back to *their* warm
beds —

... for a "dead" man.

I was alive.

Did you *stop* somewhere on the way home?

Odysseus?

Where are you going?

I will not warm this bed for you.

ODYSSEUS

Penelope!

PENELOPE

I am not your… toaster!

ODYSSEUS

My north star…

PENELOPE

It hurts, doesn't it.

ODYSSEUS

Hurts? Here's what hurts: I lost… every ship…

I lost… every man… Perimedes, Eurylochus, Elpenor, Anti-clus, Thoas… brave Achaeans, equal hearts who stood with me and strove with me, rowed with me, suffered my lash,…

Oh gods, forgive me!

I will not lose you now.

PENELOPE

And why were you tangling with monsters?

ODYSSEUS

I was curious… Penelope, men will be men… or the winds, the squalls, battering, wreaking, blowing us from charted ways… my men, suspicious, foolishly opening the Bag of

Winds — fools! cynics! secularists! Or the winds of lust, stirred within, by the unrelenting gods.

PENELOPE

Men need no gods for this.

ODYSSEUS

There was a god who ruled — praise be to his immortal name, though his will be ever obscure. We heard the cracks of his reeking bolts and every sinew froze. There were gods and goddesses to protect; they walked with us, saved us from ourselves. There were nymphs to tempt us, cattle of the Sun, and monstrous offspring to crack our bones and spit out our brains. And one god, son of Cronus and Rhea, Poseidon the Earth-Shaker, had it in for me. God against mortal, who can prevail? On sea, on land, clashing North Wind and East, cracking oaks, filling all heaven with heaving clouds, raising huge crests like hands to drag me down — I swear I once saw in the swirl of dark foam his trident-wielding fist!

You have lived your life under roofs — no fault to you. You've had your kingdoms to command. But I have lived among the elements. There I've made my kingdom, and there I've been unmade.

Forgive me if my hand feels rough against your cheek.

PENELOPE

… I know you so well. Why would the great Poseidon have it in for little you, when you have an unfading beauty for a goddess, protector, and partner in the huddle?

47

ODYSSEUS

I erred.

PENELOPE

To "err" means to wander.

ODYSSEUS

I erred in my heart. My years of wandering sprang from — do I have to tell you this?

PENELOPE

It might be good for *us*.

ODYSSEUS

Less than a year out of Troy, after we had eaten the lotus flowers that stole from us almost all desire for home —

PENELOPE

— why? —

ODYSSEUS

When men fight ten years for honor and home, a life of sweet ease — a television, a remote, a beer — is easily mistaken for the soul's desire.

We landed upon a shore and came upon the cave home of Poseidon's ghastly, one-eyed spawn. A mountain-heaving brute. To cut to the chase, we trespass, he locks us in, he barbecues and eats six of us in his hellish fire, we get him drunk, we poke his eye out with a sharp stick, more like a flag pole, I trick him into letting us out — you know me, always tricking — yada yada,… and pretty soon I'm standing on the hillside yelling down —

PENELOPE

I can guess…

ODYSSEUS

No, it's better than you think. I'd told him my name was "Nobody" —

PENELOPE

You didn't pull that one…

ODYSSEUS

Heh heh… So when he's yowling about his big blind eye — his one-eyed buddies ask who, and he tells them "Nobody" did this to me. So they thunder at him, "Then what are you complaining about?" It was hilarious. They were so stupid. You know, I've told this story so many times.

PENELOPE

But then you —

ODYSSEUS

— stood on the hill —

PENELOPE

— and said —

ODYSSEUS

— and said, "Cyclops, if any man should ask you who blinded you, who shamed you so — say Odysseus, raider of cities, *he* gouged out your eye, Laertes' son who makes his home in Ithaca."

PENELOPE

You didn't.

ODYSSEUS

I did.

PENELOPE

Oops.

ODYSSEUS

Yep, I basically gave him the map.

PENELOPE

Odysseus. You needed me there.

ODYSSEUS

Oh yeah. He would have used you for a toothpick.

PENELOPE

And then?

ODYSSEUS

Well, then, I was dealing with a mad dad the rest of the way. Polyphemus — that was his name — he threw rocks,

big ones, size of mountain peaks, you know — but he had
a terrible arm, threw like a sissy, so we laughed and rowed
hard, no problem.

But before he started tossing rocks he raised his hands to the
starry sky — night, you see, but for him what does it matter,
his eye's out — and bellowed out this horrible prayer, that
I for one will never forget, and it ought to explain a lot to
you. He says:

"Hear me, Poseidon, god of the sea-blue mane who rocks
the earth! As I am your son, come, grant that Odysseus,
raider of cities, Laertes' son who makes his home in Ithaca"
— I know, I know — "never reaches home. Or if he's fated
to see his people once again and reach his well-built house
and his own native country, let him come home late" — see,
there it is — "and come a broken man — all shipmates' lost,
alone in a stranger's ship — and let him find a world of pain
at home!"

PENELOPE

Oh!

ODYSSEUS

See? It's like they say, "Be careful what a cyclops prays for
— he might get it."

PENELOPE

I didn't know.

All came true.

All true?

ODYSSEUS

Yeah. It was… an uphill battle after that.

PENELOPE

And did you really find a world of pain at home? That sounds so horrible. I worked every day to keep it nice for you.

ODYSSEUS

Oh, yeah! The suitors and all? It was a bloody mess — which you slept through, thank god, literally. We got the whole crew after it, though — except the twelve who were whoring with the suitors — those we strung up from a wire until their heels stopped kicking. You would have been amazed at how everybody worked — gobbets of fat, severed ears, entrails, blood on the cushions — we had everything cleaned up and the incense going before you even came down.

PENELOPE

I just thought it was fantastic having somebody else clean the house. I thought: I could get used to this.

ODYSSEUS

See? There's a lot more that goes on than you know.

PENELOPE

Come back to bed, Odysseus. This is our night. Let's get back the joy.

You know what I think? I think we're just nervous.

In some strange way, I don't think you're even quite the same person — not bad, just different! And I, I think I'm in some ways different.

It's as if… we both… died. And now here we are, back at the start, and yet the world has moved on. We're playing catch-up, and it's hard.

Odysseus? Join me? Let the new moon hold the old moon in her arms.

ODYSSEUS

My heart is troubled by what I must say. Penelope,…

Penelope?

PENELOPE

Must we have complications? Peace has returned to Ithaca. The cost has been… severe.

ODYSSEUS

I must tell you —

PENELOPE

What is it, my USDA Prime specimen of manhood — is it a woman?

ODYSSEUS

Oh no —

PENELOPE

Wily one, you speak with winged words. Is it more than this jealous goddess of yours, who fills all of this room except for the bed she so much desires? Because I want to tell you that when you came in to me fresh from your bath I noted… your "enhancements." Half a head taller, amazingly buff — oh, I notice — and the hyacinthine clusters of hair, ring curls all about your shoulders, oh, you had goddess written all over you. I didn't want to say a thing and spoil the evening, but I could practically smell her Eternity perfume.

Odysseus,… Odysseus… you don't need the cosmetic thing. You're good as you are. Honey, need I convince you of that? Nobody falls for it. Here's why I'm your wife: because I DON'T CARE.

I mean, I *care*… but I don't care.

Are there others?

ODYSSEUS

Penelope. It's not —

PENELOPE

Are there others? Golden tressed nymphettes? Rippling naiads? Giggling, fat-fingered little twits? Snake-haired gorgons? Thousand-breasted wonder women? I mean, not that I care. Twenty years, I've hardened. What could you do to surprise me? But I want to know. I just want to know, because it would tell me something about you. And if it's about you, it's about us.

Ten years to war. Ten years return. You've accounted for one of those last ten. There's nine more, Charley. Who is she?

ODYSSEUS

That's not my point. My point is much more —

Okay. Okay, for the sake of clarity, for the record, — and it's over, I tell you, it's over — there was one. Circe. I was with her for a year.

PENELOPE

A year.

A year.

ODYSSEUS

Don't assume —

PENELOPE

Don't tell me what to assume. DON'T tell me.

A year. Was there a child?

ODYSSEUS

Penelope!

PENELOPE

Perhaps you enjoyed her. I have no one to blame but myself. I was not there for you in your time of need.

ODYSSEUS

Your sarcasm is wasted. She was a sorceress. A mistress of the black arts. She turned my men to swine.

55

PENELOPE

Oh, lob me the big fat softball. Were there others?

ODYSSEUS

Only by the grace of god, and magic of my own —

PENELOPE

Seven years go unaccounted for. Were there others?

ODYSSEUS

Without her aid, I would not have found my way —

PENELOPE

Are you still speaking of this spellbinding little pig farmer?
Were there others.

ODYSSEUS

An other. A nymph. Calypso. Daughter of Atlas. Seven years.

PENELOPE

Nymph: check. Seven years: check check check check check
check check.

ODYSSEUS

Seven years at the seas edge mingling my tears with the salt
surge. Tears for Penelope. Tears for home.

PENELOPE

Was she beautiful? Well, of course she was. Daughter of Atlas.

Golden-haired? Unchanging? Barbie figure?

Was she smooth? Did her joints swivel?

Did you tell her she bore a faint resemblance to your faithful wife?

Any children?

ODYSSEUS

Penelope, I wept for you daily, for our home, for our boy.

PENELOPE

Waste. All waste. Talk to the hand.

ODYSSEUS

Listen to me: she offered me e-ter-nal life, life as her husband, a life of unceasing bliss, life without disappointment, or surprise,...

PENELOPE

You should have accepted the offer. Look what poor gift I bring.

ODYSSEUS

Penelope, hear me: I turned down immortality. I had it right there in my hands.

It sings with the voice of honeybees. It weaves wondrous designs. Tendrils of the vine sport like greyhounds where it walks.

If you like perfect, there it was.

PENELOPE

Could she raise a son with you? Could she bury a father and weep? Could she wait for something she couldn't have?

ODYSSEUS

Penelope, what she wanted with all her divine heart was the one thing she couldn't have. It was the thing you can have with a word, a smile.

Me.

I never gave her my heart. Never.

I came home to what's mortal … and good… and mine.

Eternity is in love with the productions of time. So a poet will someday say.

PENELOPE

Will you go back?

ODYSSEUS

This is what it troubles my heart to say…

PENELOPE

Ah ha ha.

ODYSSEUS

I will never go back. I must fare… *forward*.

PENELOPE

Odysseus? Again?

ODYSSEUS

Again.

PENELOPE

Oh, Odysseus! Again!?

ODYSSEUS

I have had it from the prophet, Tiresias.

PENELOPE

The ancient one?

ODYSSEUS

The same.

PENELOPE

Where did he come to you?

ODYSSEUS

I went to him.

Penelope, your husband has walked among the dead.

PENELOPE

While Penelope, your wife, has walked as one dead among
the living.

ODYSSEUS

Circe, the "little pig farmer", traded me, in return for a year
of surrogate marriage — business, Penelope, business — ,

gave me my path and the promise by which I have lived these many years.

She sent me by the North Wind across the Ocean River to Persephone's Grove. From there down to the crusted, moldering House of Death. From there down by Hell's rivers of Hate and Grief, Fire and Tears, to a place where I dug a trench and made fair offerings to the dead. I poured out libations: milk, honey, mellow wine, water, glistening barley. After vows and prayers, to call Tiresias I flayed a fine black ram and poured his blood into the ditch.

Yes, you touch me. I was not dead… but I was as dead.

The shades came stumbling and gibbering — scared the *crap* out of me! — I held them off with my sword — yah! yah! — and burnt more sheep and prayed like a mad monk to Hades, King of Death's Dream Kingdom and Persephone, his dread queen.

My man Elpenor came — the dimwit fell off a roof at Circe's the day we left!

And there beside the trench kneeled my mother, dear long-lost Anticleia. With all my heart I longed to speak with her, I broke into tears, I shook with grief — but mark me, Penelope, mark me! I held *her* off until — until I could hear from Tiresias news of my journey, my journey home, to *you*.

That was my first death: death to myself.

Then Tiresias came, and the old man played out everything before my eyes — like a movie. Just the way it would happen. And it did. And then came my mother and she drank the dark blood. She asked after you. I said I had not seen you in ten, twelve years, and she played the whole freak show at Ithaca before my eyes. The suitors, the feast, your weaving, our son…

From the depth of Hell I saw your suffering, and I saw what I must do. That was my second death: death unto you.

Penelope,… I had to go… to the bottom of the world… to know my heart.

PENELOPE

Did you greet your sweet mother for me?

ODYSSEUS

I tried to throw my arms around her, three times — hah! hah! hah! — like that, and my arms passed right through. More pain to me each time. She sifted through my fingers like shadow. Not even a hug.

Why do you stare? That's how it is among the Dead. And this is how the dead stare.

Penelope? Hug me.

PENELOPE

Hug me, says the vigorous old salt. Hug me.

Have you left her?

ODYSSEUS

Left. "Left?" I never touched her.

PENELOPE

Have you left her?

ODYSSEUS

I'm here for you. Why did I die and die? For you.

PENELOPE

And who am I? Oh Bragger, I am No One, too.

I am so much older than the one you've known.
This light I shine is not my own.

Come then. Let me fold the old moon in my arms.
My absence. My man.

Hug me. Hug me. Hah! You see?

I cannot touch you. You cannot touch me.
Yet together makes one.
Together we smile.

ODYSSEUS

I have left them all.

PENELOPE

You may have them all. The whole fervent pile.

ODYSSEUS

Penelope, the word of the prophet has been true.

PENELOPE

Yes.

ODYSSEUS

And so —

PENELOPE

You must follow.

ODYSSEUS

I must follow.

PENELOPE

This is my life. Cratered and still.

ODYSSEUS

He told me that at last my death will steal upon me, a gentle, painless death, far from the sea, in ripe old age with all my people there in blessed peace surrounding. But first —

PENELOPE

Yet bright withal.

ODYSSEUS

— re-enter Poseidon. Once I've killed the suitors and cleaned up the hall — check, check — and mended the kingdom and disposed of my wealth, then forth I must go to one last labor. A difficult journey, loaded with danger, hard and long. But I must tough it out once more. I was told of signs and a place, and there I must make things right with my old foe.

PENELOPE

Your tormentor and scourge.

63

ODYSSEUS

The one. I must make fitting sacrifice: a ram, a bull and a bucking wild boar. And then to Ithaca, where I must make noble offerings to the gods who rule the unbroken skies.

PENELOPE

An adult, a very *adult* thing to do.

ODYSSEUS

Are you on?

PENELOPE

I will not waver.

Then let hopes unfold from here. If the gods do grant happiness in old age, perhaps our trials will end at last. Come, while the moon stands still, while now is now and we bathe in blessing, tell me your tales.

———————